OCT 1 6 2008

Y0-BZA-646

WORLD OF INSECTS

Earwigs

by Colleen Sexton

BELLWETHER MEDIA · MINNEAPOLIS, MN

Note to Librarians, Teachers, and Parents:

Blastoff! Readers are carefully developed by literacy experts and combine standards-based content with developmentally appropriate text.

Level 1 provides the most support through repetition of high-frequency words, light text, predictable sentence patterns, and strong visual support.

Level 2 offers early readers a bit more challenge through simple sentences, increased text load, and less repetition of high-frequency words.

Level 3 advances early-fluent readers toward fluency through increased text and concept load, less reliance on visuals, longer sentences, and more literary language.

Level 4 builds reading stamina by providing more text per page, increased use of punctuation, greater variation in sentence patterns, and increasingly challenging vocabulary.

Level 5 encourages children to move from "learning to read" to "reading to learn" by providing even more text, varied writing styles, and less familiar topics.

Whichever book is right for your reader, Blastoff! Readers are the perfect books to build confidence and encourage a love of reading that will last a lifetime!

This edition first published in 2009 by Bellwether Media.

No part of this publication may be reproduced in whole or in part without written permission of the publisher. For information regarding permission, write to Bellwether Media Inc., Attention: Permissions Department, Post Office Box 19349, Minneapolis, MN 55419.

Library of Congress Cataloging-in-Publication Data
Sexton, Colleen A., 1967–
  Earwigs / by Colleen Sexton.
    p. cm. – (Blastoff! readers) (World of insects)
  Includes bibliographical references.
  Summary: "Simple text and full color photographs introduce beginning readers to earwigs. Developed by literacy experts for students in kindergarten through third grade"–Provided by publisher.
  ISBN-13: 978-1-60014-191-1 (hardcover : alk. paper)
  ISBN-10: 1-60014-191-9 (hardcover : alk. paper)
  1. Earwigs–Juvenile literature. I. Title.

QL510.S49 2008
595.7'39–dc22   2008019872

Text copyright © 2009 by Bellwether Media Inc. BLASTOFF! READERS, TORQUE, and associated logos are trademarks and/or registered trademarks of Bellwether Media Inc.

SCHOLASTIC, CHILDREN'S PRESS, and associated logos are trademarks and/or registered trademarks of Scholastic Inc. Printed in the United States of America.

Contents

Earwigs are small, flat **insects**.

An earwig is about the size
of a peanut.

5

Earwigs get their name from a belief that they crawl into people's ears. That is not true.

There are more than 1,000 different kinds of earwigs. They live all over the world.

Earwigs need cool, damp places.
During the day they may hide
under rocks or dead trees.

8

They come out at night.

Earwigs can be dark
brown, red, or black.

Earwigs have a hard, shiny body.

antennas

Earwigs have two long **antennas**. They use their antennas to feel and smell.

Earwigs have six legs.
They can crawl fast and
climb plants.

wings

Earwigs have wings. Their
thin back wings fold together
under thick front wings.

Earwigs do not fly a lot.

cerci

Earwigs have pinchers called **cerci**. Sometimes they fight other earwigs with their cerci.

Earwigs mostly use their cerci to grab and hold food.

Earwigs can bite and chew tough food.

Earwigs eat fruit, flowers, and other parts of plants. They also eat flies, spiders, and other bugs.

19

Earwig young hatch from eggs. Earwigs take care of their young. Most insects do not.

Mother earwigs feed their young and keep them safe while they grow.

Glossary

antennas—the feelers on an insect's head; insects use their antennas to touch and smell things.

cerci—pinchers on the back of an insect; male earwigs have large, curved cerci and female earwigs have smaller, straight cerci.

insect—a small animal with six legs and a body divided into three parts; there are more insects in the world than any other kind of animal.

To Learn More

AT THE LIBRARY

Mound, Laurence. *Insect.* New York: DK Publishing, 2007.

O'Neill, Amanda. *Insects and Bugs.* New York: Kingfisher, 2002.

St. Pierre, Stephanie. *Earwig.* Chicago, Ill.: Heinemann Library, 2002.

ON THE WEB

Learning more about earwigs is as easy as 1, 2, 3.

1. Go to www.factsurfer.com

2. Enter "earwigs" into search box.

3. Click the "Surf" button and you will see a list of related web sites.

With factsurfer.com, finding more information is just a click away.

Index

antennas, 12
body, 11
bugs, 19
cerci, 16, 17
color, 10
day, 8
eggs, 20
flies, 19
flowers, 19
food, 17, 18
fruit, 19
insects, 4, 20
legs, 13
name, 6
night, 9
people, 6
pinchers, 16
plants, 13, 19
rocks, 8
size, 5

spiders, 19
trees, 8
wings, 14
world, 7
young, 20, 21

The images in this book are reproduced through the courtesy of: David Cappaert / age fotostock, front cover, pp. 12-13; arlindo71, pp. 4-5; Mercer / insects / Alamy, p. 6; Piotr Naskrecki / Getty Images, p. 7; Dave Bevan / Alamy, pp. 8-9, 20-21; Bartomeu Borrell, pp. 10-11; Semenovigor, pp. 14-15; ARCO / J. Meul / age fotostock, pp. 16-17; JUNIORS BILDARCHIV / age fotostock, pp. 18-19.